Backyard Bugs

Dancing Dragons

Dragonflies in Your Backyard

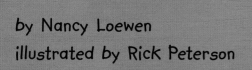

by Nancy Loewen

illustrated by Rick Peterson

Thanks to our advisers for their expertise, research, knowledge, and advice:

Blake Newton, Extension Entomologist
University of Kentucky

Susan Kesselring, M.A., Literacy Educator
Rosemount–Apple Valley–Eagan (Minnesota) School District

PICTURE WINDOW BOOKS
Minneapolis, Minnesota

Editorial Director: Carol Jones
Managing Editor: Catherine Neitge
Creative Director: Keith Griffin
Editor: Jill Kalz
Story Consultant: Terry Flaherty
Designer: Nathan Gassman
Page Production: Picture Window Books
The illustrations in this book were created with acrylics.

Picture Window Books
5115 Excelsior Boulevard
Suite 232
Minneapolis, MN 55416
877-845-8392
www.picturewindowbooks.com

Printed in the United States of America.

Library of Congress Cataloging-in-Publication Data
Loewen, Nancy, 1964–
Dancing dragons : dragonflies in your backyard / by Nancy Loewen ; illustrated by
Rick Peterson.
p. cm. — (Backyard bugs)
ISBN 1-4048-1142-7 (hardcover)
1. Dragonflies—Juvenile literature. I. Peterson, Rick, ill. II. Title.
QL520.L64 2005
595.7'33—dc22
2005004058

Table of Contents

Big-Eyed Bugs

What's that strange bug darting and gliding at the edge of the pond?

It looks like a living airplane—with very big eyes!

Now it's settled on a plant.
Let's take a closer look.

6

It's a dragonfly! It has a long, thin body, with two pairs of wings. The wings stay spread even when the dragonfly is at rest. And look at those eyes! They are so big and round that they nearly touch each other.

Dragonflies and damselflies look a lot alike. A damselfly, however, has a thinner body, and its eyes are farther apart. And when a damselfly is at rest, it folds its wings above its back.

Mating and Laying Eggs

Dragonflies mate in the air. They circle each other, and then they hook themselves together. Their bodies form a loop.

While mating, a male dragonfly holds onto a female dragonfly with special hooks on the end of his abdomen.

Soon after mating, the female dragonfly lays her eggs.

She places them on top of the water or sticks them to the stem of a water plant. A few kinds of dragonflies make small rips in the stems and put the eggs inside.

Dragonflies lay hundreds or even thousands of eggs. They help make sure that there will always be plenty of dragonflies in the world.

Dragons of the Water

In a week or two, the eggs hatch. The young dragonflies are called nymphs. They live in the water and breathe through special openings in their abdomens called gills.

A dragonfly nymph is a fierce predator. It eats bugs, tadpoles, and even small fish. It catches its food with a toothed lower lip. When a likely meal swims nearby, the nymph shoots out its lower lip with lightning speed.

Dragonfly nymphs have to watch out for enemies, too, such as fish, turtles, and water bugs.

From Water to Land to Sky

A dragonfly nymph eats and grows. It molts, or sheds its outer skin, 10 times or more.

Finally, the nymph is ready to molt for the last time. It crawls out of the water and rests on a leaf or stem. Its skin splits, and an adult dragonfly works its way out. At first, the dragonfly is crumpled and helpless. But then the dragonfly changes. Its wings spread, and its body grows longer and harder.

After spending so much of its life in the water, the dragonfly is finally ready to fly.

Some kinds of dragonflies are nymphs for several weeks before they become adults. Others are nymphs for more than four years.

A Flying Champion

Dragonflies are among the best fliers in the bug world. Their two pairs of wings move separately from each other. This separation lets dragonflies fly in special ways.

They can fly forward and backward.
They can even fly in place like a helicopter.

A dragonfly's wings are transparent, with many veins. The wings of some kinds of dragonflies have color patterns that are different for males and females.

Part of the Food Chain

While in the air, a dragonfly hunts for mosquitoes, flies, beetles, moths, and wasps. It uses its strong jaws to catch and eat prey while flying.

18

Dragonflies have many enemies, too. Birds, frogs, lizards, and spiders like to eat dragonflies—if they're lucky enough to catch them.

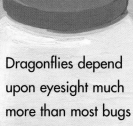

Dragonflies depend upon eyesight much more than most bugs do. Each eye has nearly 30,000 tiny lenses. A lens is the clear part of an eye that focuses light.

Back to the Beginning

After several weeks of flying and eating, dragonflies return to the pond, stream, or lake where they hatched. They mate, and the females lay eggs. The dragonflies die soon afterward.

20

But in the water, hidden from view, more dragonfly nymphs are getting ready for their turn in the sky.

21

Look Closely at a Dragonfly

Look at a dragonfly through a magnifying glass. How many of these different parts can you see?

- Long, transparent **wings** keep a dragonfly in the air.

- Each of a dragonfly's two giant **eyes** is made of lots of smaller parts.

- Like all bugs, a dragonfly has six **legs**.

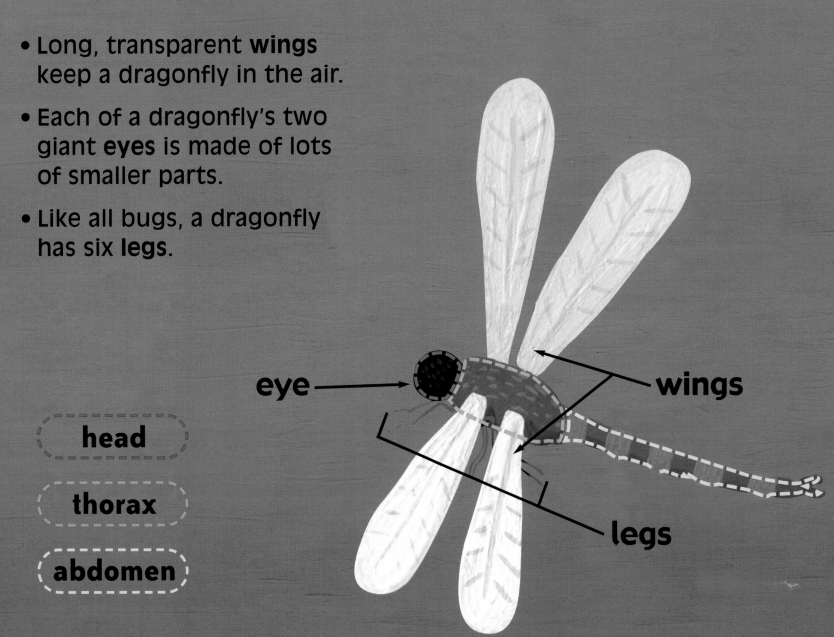

eye

wings

legs

head

thorax

abdomen

Fun Facts

- Dragonflies have been around since before the time of the dinosaurs. These ancient dragonflies measured about 30 inches (76 centimeters) across, from the tip of one front wing to the tip of the other. This distance is about the length of a little-league baseball bat.

- Dragonflies have nicknames in some parts of the world. Some people call them "snake doctors," "horse stingers," "mosquito hawks," and "devil's darning needles."

- Adult dragonflies often have bright bodies, in shades of blue, green, yellow, red, and violet. The nymphs, however, are dull in color so they can blend into their surroundings.

A Dragonfly That Won't Fly Away

Dragonflies often appear in art and jewelry. You can make your own dragonfly using everyday materials.

For the wings: Get a piece of waxed paper about the size of this book. Spread a light layer of clear-drying school glue all over it. Cut some long pieces of thread and put them on the waxed paper in interesting patterns. Next, place another piece of waxed paper over the first and press lightly. Allow the glue to dry thoroughly.

For the body: Paint a Popsicle stick a bright color, or cut out a long, narrow body from construction paper. (Gluing several layers of paper on top of one another will make the body stronger.)

For the eyes: Get two dried peas, beads, buttons, or candy. Glue them onto the head of the body.

Now, have an adult help you cut out four wings from the waxed paper, and glue them onto the body. If you have extra wing material, why not make another dragonfly?

Words to Know

abdomen – The abdomen is the last section of a bug's body.

mate – Male and female dragonflies mate by joining together special parts of their bodies. After they've mated, the female dragonfly can lay eggs.

nymphs – When dragonflies are changing from eggs to adults, they are called nymphs (NIMFS).

predators – Predators are animals that hunt other animals for food.

prey – Animals that are hunted by other animals for food are called prey.

transparent – Transparent is another word for clear. If something is transparent, you can see through it.

veins – Veins are thin tubes that help give shape to a bug's wings.

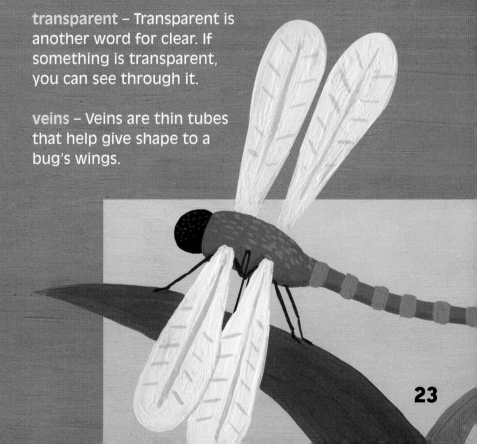

To Learn More

At the Library

Jacobs, Liza. *Dragonflies*. San Diego: Blackbirch Press, 2003.

McEvey, Shane F. *Dragonflies*. Philadelphia: Chelsea House Publishers, 2001.

Meister, Cari. *Dragonflies*. Edina, Minn.: Abdo Publishing, 2001.

On the Web

FactHound offers a safe, fun way to find Web sites related to this book.
All of the sites on FactHound have been researched by our staff.
www.facthound.com

1. Visit the FactHound home page.
2. Enter a search word related to this book, or type in this special code: 1404811427.
3. Click on the FETCH IT button.

Your trusty FactHound will fetch the best sites for you!

Look for all of the books in the Backyard Bugs series:

Busy Buzzers: Bees in Your Backyard

Bzzz, Bzzz! Mosquitoes in Your Backyard

Chirp, Chirp! Crickets in Your Backyard

Dancing Dragons: Dragonflies in Your Backyard

Flying Colors: Butterflies in Your Backyard

Garden Wigglers: Earthworms in Your Backyard

Hungry Hoppers: Grasshoppers in Your Backyard

Living Lights: Fireflies in Your Backyard

Night Fliers: Moths in Your Backyard

Spotted Beetles: Ladybugs in Your Backyard

Tiny Workers: Ants in Your Backyard

Weaving Wonders: Spiders in Your Backyard

Index

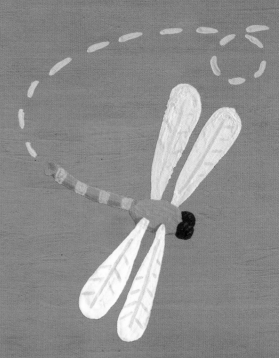